THE
TEN FETTERS

Saŋyojana

The Buddha's Doctrine of the

TEN FETTERS

BRIAN TAYLOR

道

UNIVIVERSAL OCTOPUS

Published by Universal Octopus 2016
www.universaloctopus.com

A catalogue record of this book is available from the British Library.

ISBN 978-0-9571901-1-5

CONTENTS

THE TEN FETTERS

All the Buddha's teachings, as recorded in the *Sutta Pitaka* (1), are intended to release human beings from all forms of suffering and reawaken them to a permanent, deathless state of peace and happiness.

Put simply, his message is that man has gone astray through thinking wrong thoughts and doing wrong actions. If he painstakingly purifies himself, he will be back on track for the ultimate goal, Nibbāna. As it is recorded in the *Dhammapada,* "All Buddhas teach the same thing: Don't do evil; cultivate good; purify the mind."

Saṇyojana* means "mental fetter, chain". The Ten Fetters translated here are those found in the *Sutta Pitaka.* There is a different set in the *Abhidhamma.*

A fetter is something that holds you down as a prisoner so that you lose your freedom and power to escape. Except in the case of masochists, fetters are applied by others.

In Buddhist psychology, we are shown that the Saṇyojanas come from *within* ourselves. Escape is not really a matter of breaking free of the fetters but of letting go our grasp on them.

---

* Saṇyojana: pronounced "sangy*o*chana". ("*o*" as in "h*o*pe")

These are the TEN FETTERS:

1. Sakkāya-ditthi

2. Vicikicchā

3. Sīlabbata-parāmāsā

4. Kāma raga

5. Vyāpāda

6. Rūpa-rāga

7. Arūpa-rāga

8. Māna

9. Uddhacca

10. Avijjā

1. Sakkāya-ditthi:

"Own body views".

In the commentaries, which are all later than the Buddha's teachings, it is said that sakkāya corresponds to *sat-kāya,* "existing group" and not to Sanskrit *sva-kāya,* "own group" or "own body".

However, it makes better sense to see it as equivalent to sva + kāya = "own" + "body", where "body" refers to both the physical body and the mental body.

In most English versions, sakkāya-ditthi (2) is translated as "personality belief" but this is too imprecise and tends to suggest to western students that they don't exist, which they often don't find very helpful.

What is meant is that any opinions (views) about the mind and body complex make one think of it as some kind of self or possession. Since mind-body is the source of all suffering, one will never achieve liberation from it while one hangs on to opinions about it; such as it is oneself or can be possessed by oneself. With thoughts like these, one will never entirely let go of attachment to mind-body. What is required is investigation of how mind-body is constructed in terms of the five khandhas (3). Full understanding of these is followed by letting go.

2. **Vicikicchā**:

"Doubt".

This is always translated as "doubt in the Buddha's Teachings". It certainly includes this doubt. But it actually refers to any doubts.

Think about it: The fetters are almost as old as the Saŋsāra* (4) and men have been releasing themselves and becoming enlightened since long before the Buddha and his teaching appeared.

Until one has completely freed oneself from all attachment to existence, one will constantly have doubts about all kinds of things; livelihood, the way of the world, relationships, past and future. All these exist only in the Saŋsāra. It is like living in a prison. Should one paint the walls, change the curtains, install carpets, rearrange the room, make improvements?

Once one is convinced that it is a prison and that one is holding the key in one's hand, one makes straight for the door to escape.

---

* Saŋsāra: pronounced "Sangsāra".

3. Sīlabbata-parāmāsā:

"Clinging to the practice of morality".

This is almost everywhere translated as "attachment (clinging) to mere rules (rites) and rituals".

There is nothing in the Pali which corresponds to "mere". This is a word which is used to belittle something (a *mere* actor; the *merest* trace). You cannot have "mere" morality. The use of it indicates that the translators have not understood the meaning of the words, the intention in the meaning and the nature of morality.

Sīlabbata = sīla + bata ("bata" comes from earlier "vata").
sīla = "morality, character, behaviour".
vata = "practice, custom, behaviour".
parāmāsā = "attachment, clinging, misapprehension".

Sīlabbata-parāmāsā means "clinging to the practice of morality".

Fetters are bonds which hold one down. In Buddhist psychology, fetters do not hold *us* down; it is we who hold on to *them.*

Like a man who is stuck at the bottom of the sea because he is holding on to a heavy anchor.

It is the *clinging* to morality which creates the fetter. Just as it is the clinging to the heavy anchor which stops the man from escaping from the seabed. The key word is "clinging".

There is nothing wrong with morality, including many conventional codes of good conduct. When beings become enlightened, they certainly do not give up morality. One should never denigrate it by calling it *mere* morality.

However, all morality is practised *within* the field of the Saŋsāra. If you *escape from* the Saŋsāra, there is nowhere to practise morality, nor any need for the mental concepts of "morality" or "practising".

If on the other hand you cling to your practice of morality, deriving satisfaction from your behaviour, allowing an opinion of yourself to arise (see first fetter) such as "I am one who practises morality", then this clinging will produce rebirth where more morality can be practised. That is, within the Saŋsāra. But rebirth within the Saŋsāra is always accompanied by sickness, old age and death. In other words, the whole range of Suffering.

It is true that you cannot escape from the Saŋsāra unless your morality is perfect (avoid bad; do good; purify the mind) but it is also true you can't escape suffering if you keep coming back to the Saŋsāra and being reborn. Hence the fetter.

4. **Kāma-rāga**:

"Desire for sense objects".

The senses contact a sense object. This causes feelings to arise. The feelings can be pleasant, unpleasant or neutral. If the feeling is pleasant, it can give rise to strong desire and clinging. It is this *clinging* that constitutes the fetter. It binds you down to the Saŋsāra where all these desirable sense objects exist and so you come back again and again in order to experience them. You can't escape because you keep coming back.

It is not only sexual lust (as in most translations) which is meant. It is *any* sense contacting *any* sense object. Think of those Roman gluttons who, having eaten as much as they could, took an emetic, vomited it all up and returned to the table! Think of the youngsters going everywhere with earphones full of music. Think of Cleopatra and her vials of perfume.

5. **Vyāpāda**:

"Ill-will".

Ill-will is a spectrum of feeling ranging from the slightest irritation to blind hatred. These produce corresponding thoughts, words and deeds. Irritation is the acorn, hatred the fully-grown oak. When the contact of a sense base with a sense object results in an unpleasant sensation; vyāpāda can arise. Unwise reflection on a *pleasant* object and the associated feeling can result in attraction and attachment. Unwise reflection on an *unpleasant* object can result in repulsion.

In either case, clinging is the result and a fetter is created which binds you to the level on which these objects exist, i.e. the Saŋsāra. If you go back to a room to meet your lover or to settle accounts with your enemy, in either case you go back to the same room - the room of birth and death.

6. **Rūpa-rāga**:

"Desire for Form".

"Rūpa" means "form". Rāga means "desire". (In the compound nāma-rūpa, rūpa means "matter" when contrasted with "mind").

In physical matter, rūpa can refer to a distinct shape which appears to the mind as a separate recognisable object. If it is something living, this can be a man, a tree, a flower etc. In matter which is not living, it can be a recognisable form such as a statue, a rock, a lake, a building, a photograph etc.

Rūpa-rāga at this level can be desire for anything seen which is recognised by the mind and stimulates desire and attachment. It may also be accompanied by kāma-rāga as in the case of the *Rokeby Venus*. Or it may not, if the attraction is aesthetic: Constable's *Hay Wain* or the view from the bedroom window. It may also be for things heard, e.g. a Beethoven symphony.

Where there is no kāma-rāga, it is clear that the attachment is for the *perceived* form which is superimposed by the mind on a physical sankhāra (6) made up of the four elements. In the cinema the desire is not for the screen but for the scene projected on it. That is to say, the *Rokeby Venus* is not a real woman, she is just a picture on a canvas. Often, this is not realised. In such a case, if the physical object is destroyed, the form disappears and unpleasant feelings, in proportion to attachment to the *form*, are experienced as though something real had actually been lost. In the case of this particular picture, a reproduction could just as easily compensate for the aesthetic loss. Apart from that, any loss is merely financial because of its perceived equivalent in money or because of an idea that the original material, made up of molecules and atoms, is of more significance than an exact copy of the projected form.

Those who can see very clearly the *distinction* between the collection of physical elements and the mentally superimposed image, choose the image. It is less obviously impermanent. In the *Hay Wain*, which is a picture, the seasons do not change; there are no gadflies, no smells of horse manure, and no unwelcome sounds. The worst that can happen is that the canvas itself can be destroyed. If one goes one stage further and dispenses with the canvas, retaining the imagery solely in the mind, one detaches it altogether from matter. Moreover a *mental* facsimile can be made of an object without its imperfections and without its transience.

One can also improve it. One can choose to view it in spring or in a snowstorm. One can people it with one's friends. One can introduce motion and background music from the *Pastoral Symphony*. One can bring it alive. *One can enter it.*

At this point one is effectively creating a heaven world, a private inner garden in which "moth and rust doth not corrupt nor do thieves break in and steal". Anyone, using a combination of imagination (the creation of images i.e. *rūpas*) and concentration, can do this.

Hence the *Forms*, the pictures, the *rūpas*, can in their turn become the basis for clinging, either to forms associated with the elements (i.e. the material Saŋsāra) or to forms dissociated from the elements (i.e. heaven worlds). In either case, one is drawn back to the objects of one's desire. One is drawn back to be born again on the plane of existence on which they exist. And to die again.

7. **Arūpa-rāga**:

"Desire for the formless."

A + rūpa means "without form".

The arūpakhandhas (5) are feeling, perception, (mental) sankhāras (6) and consciousness. These can also become the objects of clinging.

There are four arūpa-jhānas (7). These are the four highest states of meditation in which there is no perception of, or consciousness of, form. Beings who succeed in achieving any of these find them more satisfactory than physical existence or even existence in the heaven worlds of form. When they die, they generally arise in the plane of existence which corresponds to the particular jhāna they have attained. Life on these arūpa planes is very long. The Buddha's two former teachers are still there. They arose there because they did not achieve anything higher during their lifetimes. They thought this was the ultimate. But on these planes, too, you arise (get born) and, after a time, you fall away from them (die) and are born again somewhere else as the result of latent, unfulfilled karma. More birth, more death.

Birth and death are the characteristics of all planes of existence except Nibbāna, which is the highest.

Hence, although there is no suffering in these states or these worlds, the fact that they are impermanent makes them unsatisfactory and the desire for them constitutes a fetter.

Even for non-meditators, when one just sits and thinks, the actual *process* of thinking is formless. What one thinks *about* may be objects of sense. The desire for these will be kāma-rāga.

Where the delight is for thinking about *forms* perceived through the eye or ear it will be rūpa-rāga.

However, certain types of thinking, where the mind is quite detached and without feelings, either for or against the content of the thoughts, are arūpa. Pure mathematics is arūpa; for example when one is thinking about *numbers* and not relating them to actual objects (forms). That is, one is not thinking of five apples divided among three people, but simply 5 divided by 3.

8. **Māna**:

"Conceit".

This is generally translated as "conceit" or "pride". "Conceit" means "an exalted conception of self-worth". *Māna* can be both gross and subtle. It appears as *asmimāna,* the conceit of "I am": i.e. "I exist as a separate physical or mental entity". It is an underlying tendency (*anusaya*) to compare oneself with others in ways where one is identifying oneself with own mind or own body.

Comparison is in itself not a fetter. I can say, "I am bigger than he is or older or speak more French." But these may be simple conventional matters of fact, similar to "He has red hair, I have brown" or even "His hair is redder than mine". It is when I *identify* with something which may or may not be a fact, but which I *grasp after* as in some way belonging to me personally, that the fetter arises.

It arises in three forms: I am better than him; I am equal to him; I am not as good as him. Each of these may be matters of fact. However, one needs to be aware of the mental state that accompanies them to see if there is any trace of self-exaltation or self-satisfaction. One often meets people who are insistent that they are not as good as someone (Jesus perhaps. Or Joe DiMaggio). This may well be true but, if they take undue satisfaction in their humility, it will, on examination, be found to be not humility at all but inverted pride.

It is clear that *māna* depends upon duality. Ultimately, everything is a unity. We are all part of the whole whether we realise this or not. One can visualise the whole universe as an octopus and living beings as the tentacles. One can see that, fundamentally, under the influence of *māna*, a tentacle is comparing itself to another tentacle.

"There being really no duality, pluralism is untrue."

The *fetter* consists in being bound to (holding on to) a secondary level of being, the level of duality.

9. **Uddhacca**:

"Restlessness".

This is a state of mind which is agitated and scattered. The image given is of a layer of dust which has been stirred up or a bowl of still water into which more water is poured so that ripples go out in all directions.

Whenever the mind is working, it is moving. This in itself is not a problem. What creates the *fetter* is when it is out of control. As one discovers when one tries to stop it. Since "mind comes first" and everything which is to be done starts with the mind, one cannot overestimate the seriousness of this.

When one says it is "out of control", one usually means it is out of *one's* control. The dust doesn't stir itself up. Nor does the water agitate itself. So what *does* control the mind? Associative thinking (one thought leading to another), feelings, memories, desires, sense objects appearing at the sense doors (one hears something or sees something or smells something or one's body itches or hurts). The list is endless. Many things can (and do) take control of what one thinks of as one's own mind.

This is why one so rarely moves smoothly towards an intended goal. It is as though one sets off to drive somewhere but other people keep trying to grab the steering wheel and steer off in different directions.

Uddhacca is also listed as a hindrance to meditation. One can't make progress in meditation if one can't control the mind and keep it focussed on the meditation object.

So, whether one is a meditator or just someone who wants to bring his mind under control in ordinary everyday life, it is essential to deal with this fetter.

There are two ways of doing this; both equally difficult. With the first, one forces the mind to focus on a single, chosen object. With the other, one patiently undertakes the task of observing the mind and its workings in order to thoroughly understand *how* it operates. One's growing understanding is then used to gradually bring it under control. Both methods require patience and perseverance. But the rewards of success are enormous.

One can see that some people find this easier than others. This is because the more one has neglected one's mind; the harder it is to put it to rights. If a gardener goes off for a couple of years, what he finds when he comes back will appear daunting. "Nature" has taken over. Neglect of one's mind may have lasted much longer than a couple of years! Kamma is perfect.

10. **Avijjā**:

"Not seeing things as they actually are."

Vijjā is cognate with English "vision". It means "seeing" and also "understanding what you see". In this case, it means seeing the world and everything in it as it actually is, without projecting viewpoints upon what you are looking at which make it appear otherwise. In other words, "correct seeing" or "right view." Seeing correctly includes seeing unsatisfactory things as unsatisfactory and satisfactory things as satisfactory.

Avijjā means not seeing things as they actually are. Not seeing unsatisfactory things as unsatisfactory.

Avijjā (8) appears as the first step in the *Dependent Origination**. It is also the primary fetter. If we see unsatisfactory things as in some way satisfactory, then we cling to them and make of them a fetter. This fetter binds us to the level of unsatisfactory things; the level on which beings experience birth, sickness, old age and death. That is, it keeps us in the Saŋsāra. Forever.

---

* See *Dependent Origination*
http://stores.lulu.com/wormseyeview

CONCLUSION

If we have succeeded in releasing ourselves from all ten fetters we are Arhats. If we haven't, we can use them as a tool to see and identify those things which arise in the mind and keep us trapped in a world of suffering. We can patiently weaken their hold on us (which is our hold on them) and, ultimately, free ourselves from them forever.

NOTES

(1) Sutta Pitaka:

Pitaka means "basket" and therefore "collection". The Sutta Pitaka is the collection of discourses in the Pali language given by the Buddha and his senior Disciples during his lifetime. They therefore represent the most authentic form of what is called "Buddhism". Since his Parinibbāna (death), there have been many additions and changes of direction and they are still going on. Buddhism has been continuously "updated" or adjusted to contemporary ideas or "allowed to develop" and has, in some cases, evolved in ways which make it unrecognisable.

The Sutta Pitaka is Basic Buddhism and is the reference point for anyone who wants to know what the Buddha actually taught. So that he can put it into practice and make an end of suffering.

(2) Sakkāya-ditthi:

The Buddha taught that all things are not-self. He said that if we examine all the physical and mental bits which seem to make up "I" they will be seen like the parts of a chariot – the wheels, the shaft, the axle, the seat etc. "Chariot" is just the name given to the totality of its parts when they are together and function in a certain way. When they are taken apart and removed, there is nothing left over of the "chariot". It is the same with "I". It is just a name, useful in a conventional world.

But one can hardly go around saying to people, "I don't exist!"

This is how the Buddha said we should answer if we are asked about ourselves:

"I *was* in the Past but what I was, I am not Now.

I *am* Now but what I am, I was not in the Past and I will not be in the Future.

I *will be* in the Future but what I will be, I am not Now and I was not in the Past." *

What does this mean?

It means; the man who gets off the train is not the same man as the man who crosses the platform. Yet another man gets on a different train.

That's the problem. *Now* I see things one way. I understand very clearly. I make a decision. Tomorrow's man inherits this. But his viewpoint, feelings and understanding *then* are likely to be different from *mine* now. He may come to a different conclusion. If he does, he will make a different decision.

Each "I" is like a bead on a string. The beads make a continuous row but each bead is separate.

---

* Dīgha Nikāya Poṭṭhapāda Sutta

Each new self succeeds the previous one with great rapidity.

Each self comes complete with feelings, understanding, and viewpoints. The string itself represents desire and vipāka kamma (9). Vipāka kamma means kamma left over from the past. Each bead conditions, but is different from, the next one.

While there is body to provide a reference point, this constant appearance of new selves is not usually so obvious. So one gets the impression that there is a *someone there* who changes. But this is incorrect.

And there is no shortage of selves who intermittently understand very well what *should* be done, which trains to get on and which to avoid. But they are often succeeded by other selves, in the same body, who don't actually *do* it. And still other selves who see things quite differently again.

What's the answer? One has to work until one really *does* understand something. 100 percent. Then one has to make an effort to fix this understanding in the endless flow of selves so that, although the selves continue to change, this decision is constantly inherited by each in its turn and is always there.

The effort to fix it is called in Buddhism, adhitthāna. This is usually translated as "determination" But this is not practical enough.

Literally it means "place, foundation". That gives us a clue. If you use something as a foundation, everything you build on it remains durable and in place. Even if you keep changing the superstructure, the foundation remains constant. If you make an adhitthāna about something, all the succeeding selves rest on it and inherit it. So it appears as a foundation for each of them. The Buddha made an adhitthāna under the bodhi tree to the effect that he would sit there until he had either found the truth or died. He also made adhitthānas before each of his last ten births as to which of the Perfections he intended to perfect in that lifetime.

(3) Khandhas:

The "groups" or "categories" which make up existence. These are the five aspects in which the Buddha categorised all the physical and mental phenomena of existence, leaving no room for a separately existing permanent self or ego. These categories are form, feeling, perception, sankhāras (6) and consciousness. What is called individual existence is in reality nothing but a procession of these mental and physical phenomena, a process which has been going on since time immemorial and will continue after death for unthinkably long periods of time.

(4) Saŋsāra:

Literally "endless wandering"; the sea of life, forever restless, heaving up and down; the round of birth and death and rebirth; the unbroken chain of the khandhas, continually changing from moment to moment through inconceivable periods of time. Seeing this as it is, one sees the fearsomeness of it. One sees the First Noble Truth, the Truth of Suffering. One understands the necessity of escaping from it and finding lasting peace and happiness.

(5) Arūpakhandhas:

The Khandhas (see (3)) minus the first one, "form".

(6) Sankhāras:

A sankhāra is a compound. Something made up of bits. Not a thing in itself. If you take away all the bits, there is nothing left over. Like a motor car. Apart from all the parts, put together in a certain way, there is no car. Just the idea of a car.

Everything, mental and physical, is a sankhāra, except Nibbāna.

If you can see everything that arises in the world and in your mind like this, then you are seeing it with Vijjā. If you see any of these sankhāras as things in themselves, existing as separate entities rather than as part of the flow of kamma (cause and effect), then you are seeing the world and the mind from the point of view of Avijjā.

(7) Jhānas:

The equivalent of Buddhist/Sanskrit Dhyāna. These are states of meditative absorption which start with the achievement of 100 percent concentration in which the mind no longer wanders. In the jhānas of "form" (rūpa-jhānas), the mind is progressively purified by the elimination of thought, rapture and joy until it reaches a state of equanimity beyond pleasure and pain. In the "formless" jhānas (arūpa-jhānas), the purification process is continued until the perception is, successively, wholly of Infinite Space, Infinite Consciousness, Nothingness and Neither Perception nor Non-perception. At the stage of Neither Perception nor Non-perception, the mind has withdrawn entirely from all possible worlds and levels of experience. There remains only one further stage and this is Nibbāna. Nibbāna is the only permanent state. All the others, however desirable, are not. They have a beginning and an end.

(8) Avijjā:

Everywhere this is translated as "Ignorance", especially "Ignorance of the Four Noble Truths". Ignorance means not knowing. *Knowledge* refers to data which is retained in the mind. It can be factually correct, "I know your aunt. I know the French for 'thank you'." It can be incorrect, "I know 2+2 = 5". In the latter case you do know *something*; it just happens to be wrong. *Ignorance* is simply *not knowing*. "I don't know your aunt. I don't know any French. I don't know 2+2 = anything."

Vijjā is usually translated as "Knowledge". But Vijjā is *different* from Knowledge. It is not just data retained in the mind. It means actually *seeing* in the present and, therefore, having immediate understanding of something in the present.

Many Buddhists *know* the Four Noble Truths. They can repeat them in the way a child can repeat its nine times table. They are certainly not ignorant of them. But this knowledge is not sufficient to remove Avijja as the first step in the *Dependent Origination*. It cannot thereby bring about the psychological process which the Buddha experienced under the Bodhi tree and by which he achieved Enlightenment. On the contrary, most Buddhists, who are fluent in their knowledge of the First Noble Truth, cannot even see that the food on their plates got there as the result of being bred in captivity and killed, usually painfully. They cannot see Suffering in its entirety.

So Vijjā is *not* Knowledge and Avijjā is *not* Ignorance.

Consider this example. I know there are cobras in the vicinity. I have been told this by my neighbours and I believe them. I have seen pictures of them. I have seen them in the zoo. I even know that they get into houses and there could, in theory, be one in my house. Compare this collection of knowledge with actually going into my bedroom now and seeing, on the bed, a cobra, with its hood raised, watching me as I come through the door. True seeing and understanding of this event and its relevance to me would be immediate and effective. I would not speculate on which of the several species of cobras, which can be distinguished by variations in their markings, this one might be. Nor would I attempt to measure it with a tape in order to assist identification (by relating this datum with other data in my mind). On the contrary, I should leave the room quickly and close the door behind me.

So it is with Vijjā. Seeing the First Noble Truth means seeing suffering wherever it appears, immediately and with direct, decisive understanding; the corpse on the plate, the screaming child, the widow at the funeral, the old man crying silently as he dies. Avijjā means *not seeing* these things with immediate understanding in the present, wherever they appear.

Knowledge means just knowing things as facts, stored mentally in the memory banks together with "the sun rises in the east", "a jellyfish sting can be unpleasant", "Christmas Day celebrates the birth of Jesus, although it is believed he was born on an altogether different day". Ignorance means not even knowing the facts (i.e. not having these data in the mind).

(9) Vipāka kamma:

Vipāka means *"fruit, result, consequence"*.
Kamma = Sanskrit *"karma"*.
Kamma/karma means *"doing"*, *"action"*.
Its opposite is *not doing, no action*.

So Vipāka kamma is the result, appearing in the present, of things done in the past. Everything which is done, proceeds by cause and effect. I drop the cup, it breaks. I press the switch, the light comes on.

Nothing is random. If I sow carrot seeds, I get carrots. I don't get parsnips. If I press the wall next to the switch, the light doesn't come on.

All around us in the world and inside us in our minds what we see are the effects of innumerable causes. The houses we live in, the people we associate with, environmental problems, the clothes we wear, the thoughts and memories we have, our ideas and opinions, our physical fitness. We can recognise a lot of this. Buddhism takes it further and says all phenomena are the results of causes.

But the effects of causes are also the causes of future effects. I make a sculpture. From this I make a mould. The mould is used to make more sculptures. The carrots grow; their seed will produce more carrots. My thoughts are the cause of more thoughts, or words, or actions. Cause and effect are two aspects of the same thing seen at different points in time. This is kamma. It is crucial in the realm of ethics. Just as a good seed produces a good plant, so a good deed means a good result.

Those who cannot see the connection between cause and effect are often too hasty. Like the small boy who, hearing that an acorn would grow into an oak tree, planted his acorn and came back a week later looking for his oak tree. "It doesn't work," he said.

Here and now we are surrounded by a world of effects. Here and now everything we think and say and do acts as a cause and will produce corresponding effects. We are free to choose. We have inherited the past. We can create a future we would like to inherit. Starting with our own thoughts and intentions.

Fundamental to this process is; do good, get good; do bad, get bad.

The Sun shines
in a bucket of water
and doesn't
get wet.

www.ingramcontent.com/pod-product-compliance
Lightning Source LLC
Chambersburg PA
CBHW020446030426
42337CB00014B/1421